T his book holds a very special place in my heart. I believe that you don't need to lose yourself to find yourself. But when it happens, I think that you have the duty to share the fruits of your learning experience with others. So that they too can grow and give to others.

# FULLY
# CHARGED

Plug into your 5 charging stations to feel alive,
guilt-free and unstoppable. Finally.

**STEPHANIE SEBAG**

# FULLY CHARGED

Plug into your 5 charging stations to feel alive,
guilt-free and unstoppable. Finally.

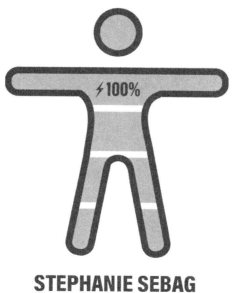

## STEPHANIE SEBAG

Illustration credits: https://www.onlinewebfonts.com/icon/411521
https://stock.adobe.com/

Published by Best Seller Publishing®, St. Augustine, FL
Best Seller Publishing® is a registered trademark.
Printed in the United States of America.
ISBN: 978-1-956649-72-7

For more information, please write:
Best Seller Publishing®
53 Marine Street
St. Augustine, FL 32084
or call 1 (626) 765-9750
Visit us online at: www.BestSellerPublishing.org

# Preface

We all go through hard times in life. For some of us, it is temporary, and for some of us, it is one crisis after another.

The last two years gave everyone an opportunity to find the strength to overcome a pandemic. This book is meant to help you answer one question after any crisis is over:

Where do I start?

What happened was real and it was not nothing. The question is, what will you do with it?

We will use what you have learned over this period of time and what you went through to realign yourself. That will allow you to go from survival mode to living mode.

You will learn to connect to what is important to you and build very solid foundations for yourself and those you love.

In order to move forward, we have to go inward.

Ready? Let's start

# Table of Contents

# To find what you are looking for you first need to know what you are looking for

In front of a complex and unusual situation, it doesn't matter if it's a small challenge, a big crisis, or even a pandemic, we instinctively revert to crisis mode and operate like a robot.

After resisting the new situation, we then accept it and finally face it.

Along the way, we have put aside our emotions in order to be able to deal, not only with what is in front of us, but also what might be coming at us.

Our only goal is to manage the risk. While our obsession is to wait for the crisis to be over, we are lost when it finally ends.

No direction, no energy.

Each human being has three primary needs:

A need for purpose, a need for belonging and a need for engagement.

When all three conditions are met, we are basically happy.

The first step in the process of experiencing happiness is to create a direction.

# Direction

D irection is a movement from the inside to the outside.

In order to move forward, we first have to move inward to create an alignment within.

The goal of every human being is to develop their potential and transform it into a reality. It is a movement from our inner-self to our reality. That's why we start with the "in" part of our-selves, where our potential is craving to go out.

Have you ever experienced a tension within yourself?

This tension comes from the difference that exists between what you think, what you say and what you do. I want to say something but I am saying something else, I am thinking this but I am doing the opposite…

Harmony, on the other hand, happens when "thinking", "saying," and "doing" are in alignment.

Like everything important, this takes practice. The first step in this process is to be aware of what is happening inside of us.

If you feel a tension, don't dismiss it. And practice understand-ing what is not in alignment. Did you do something that you never thought you would do? Are you saying something that you don't believe in?

It takes time to practice understanding what is not in alignment.

In order to achieve its potential, every human needs to align or realign themselves by putting the Mind above the Emotions, and the Emotions above the Instincts.

This alignment is the goal of achieving a happy life. When you are in survival mode, you perform with instinct first and foremost. To be able to protect yourself and your surroundings.

Now that it is time to build your life post-pandemic, it is also time to open yourself up to a new paradigm.

Why? Because you are now moving beyond relying on instinct alone and engaging your full body and soul.

By gaining access to the energy of your soul, you have access to an unlimited supply of energy.

Once you practice this alignment, it becomes second nature. At the end of this book, you will find your personal notebook to write what you observe and start identifying what is not in alignment.

With this alignment, you create harmony within yourself. And with this harmony, you have a clear direction.

It starts with the right mindset.

# Clarity in words brings clarity in actions

"If words of command are not clear and distinct,
if orders are not thoroughly understood, then
the General is to blame. But, if orders are clear
and the soldiers nevertheless disobey, then
it is the fault of their officers." —Sun Tzu

Let's start by checking in with what is actually in our brain.

# Do not confuse
# *Choices* with *Decisions*

In crisis mode, we don't have that many choices. We have to react in the moment. However, in a post-crisis life, we have the time to think through our decisions, and we can take advantage of this time.

We make all kinds of decisions for ourselves, with others, or for others. So, it is worth taking the time to talk about it.

To begin with, we need to accept that not all our decisions will be correct. Inevitably, we will sometimes be wrong. And that's ok. We also need to realize that if we don't make a decision, someone will make one for us. And we might not like it. Finally, when we don't make a decision, that, in itself, is a decision.

There will be decisions that are more important than others. It is smart to start practicing making decisions on small things and have a conversation with ourselves about it. We can learn so much about ourselves. What did I have in mind when I made this decision? What was my intention? What did I try to avoid?

When we find ourselves in a situation where we need to make a deci-sion, a tension naturally arises in us. This tension stays until the decision has been made.

If we focus on the uncomfortable feeling this tension causes, we may make a decision impulsively just to get rid of the feeling. As such, we are not focusing on the decision itself, and thus, the decision is rushed.

 However, when we accept the tension and stay with the problem until we can make the best possible decision, we can engage our full minds on the decision at hand. As a result, we gain perspective and clarity. We can then accept all the con-sequences because we took the time and created a space of reflection in order to make the best possible decision.

When we invest time getting to know, developing, and improv-ing our decision process, we can create a much simpler life for ourselves and the people we love.

Along the way, we can learn from every experience, good or bad, and it makes us stronger.

At the end of this book, there is a place for you to write notes and start observing how you make your decisions.

 "It's our choices that show what we truly are, far more than our abilities." —J.K.Rowling

Acceptance of
tension

Compassion
+
Wisdom

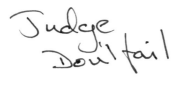

# Do not confuse
# *Learning* with *Failing*

Life is not linear. Sometimes everything goes as you want and you feel like a winner, and sometimes it is the opposite, and you feel that you have failed.

The only way to fail in life is not to try anything.

When a project does not go as you wish, when you don't have the expected outcome, this is not *Failing*. This is *Learning*.

*Learning* about yourself, about others, about many different subjects.

When everything goes well, you rarely learn anything, but you build self-confidence. That self-confidence is the strong foundation you need when things don't turn out as expected.

That foundation allows you not to believe that you have to prove yourself over and over again. That foundation enables you to accept the setback, learn from it and move on to your next project.

 "Sometimes you win and sometimes you learn." — John C. Maxwell

# Do not confuse the *Passenger seat* with the *Driver seat*

After a situation that did not go well and triggered you, you can find yourself saying: "I don't know what happened to me" or "I couldn't help myself."

When you start thinking about how you acted, you feel that you don't recognize this person. And it makes sense. We have two people inside of us: the *Driver* and the *Passenger*.

The *Driver* is the adult version of ourselves, the one who knows what is right. That's why they are driving and then next to them there is also a *Passenger*, the child version of ourselves, the one who wants to be entertained. They do not need to concentrate on the road and they are not responsible if anything happens to the car or the people around us. This child is very interested in choosing the music and bringing snacks. This child is fun to be with. But this child never learned to drive a car. This child is just going with the flow and wants to have as much fun as possible. When we find ourselves saying, "I couldn't help myself," chances are, this child wanted to learn how to drive and grabbed the steering wheel impulsively instead of staying in the *Passenger Seat.*

"A failure is always on the passenger seat in his or her life." —Stephen Richards

*Parts*

# Do not confuse
# *I have to* with *I should*
# with *I want to*

*I* *have to*, *I should* and *I want to* are noise makers playing in our heads and affecting our peace of mind.

When opportunities arise, we often doubt or have second thoughts.

We want to move forward and this doubt creates inertia. We don't want to make a mistake. We don't want to miss anything. We are pulled in different directions.

What is really happening between Should I do this? Do I have to do this? Do I want to do this?

This tension in ourselves is a good indicator of how many people inside of us are interested in making this decision for us.

"Do I really want to do this?" is the first question we need to ask our own selves. Why? Because we need to identify who wants to drive our car. Is it the child or the adult? It can be driven by the one in the passenger seat when it is about an impulse or by the adult in us when it is constructive.

It is essential to start building the relationship between the adult and the child in us as quickly as possible to create a productive dynamic between these two. If not, there are opposing forces continually debating in our heads, making it hard to make a decision. Achieving this helps us be better prepared when we eventually form a partnership, personal or professional.

After this, we should take the time to ask ourselves, "why should I do this" and "why shouldn't I do this."

Who would be happy about this decision? Would anyone be upset about it? What would be the real consequences for me if I say no? What would be the outcome if I say yes? Is this decision in alignment with my values?

We all have a Pleaser inside of us who is always ready to be activated. The one who is looking for validation or the one always happy to put their needs after everyone else's. This Pleaser is very sensitive to the entourage's expectations of them.

Finally, we can clarify with ourselves: Do I have to do this because it is important for me? Is it part of things that were urgent and that I did not address in a timely manner? Now that they became a crisis I don't have any other choice than to deal with these things.

 "Everything you've ever wanted is sitting on the other side of your fear." —George Addair

Meet our "firefighter"

# Do not confuse
# *Building* with *Improvising*

Life in crisis mode requires an on-demand availability and also readiness. You are constantly on guard and, at the same time, in constant improvisation in front of a situation. The succession of crises or a single crisis requires flexibility. The "go with the flow" mode brings the perfect answer. It brings success.

However, this mode is tactical. In order to manage the risk, we are changing direction all the time.

Life needs to be built with a strategic vision and direction.

When thinking about what we want in life, and how we will approach it, we actually can have a very happy and meaningful life. We can also overcome all the challenges along the way, and avoid creating a situation where we will have to react on the spot.

The ability to solve a crisis is a very useful skill. But creating a crisis is not necessary, and the ability to prevent one is another skill that we can develop.

Solving one crisis after another creates a busy life, not necessarily a meaningful life.

When we start realizing that we love being the firefighter of our lives because of how we feel after, we are able to slowly move away from the unconscious habit of creating a crisis and then solving it. Next thing we know, we are ready to trade this adrenaline for peace of mind.

We are looking for peace of mind.

We need this incredible firefighter in us. But not all the time. The builder in us also has to participate. And sometimes, ask the firefighter to stop starting fires that he knows he has the skills to extinguish.

Pausing to think ahead of a situation beforehand creates a space for options. And in this space, we can access the behavior that will serve us in the long term. One situation at a time.

"My goal is to build a life
I don't need a vacation
from!" —Rob Hill Sr

# Do not confuse
# *Urgent* with *Important*

**A**lthough they seem very similar, *Urgent* and *Important* are very different. President Dwight D. Eisenhower created a famous matrix to prioritize tasks widely used nowadays.

The idea behind it was to define *Urgent* as what is coming at us, while *Important* as what we want to achieve.

Let's take a look at how we spend our time.

If we find ourselves spending most of our time dealing with what is *Urgent*, chances are, we will only react to events in our life. We can easily get stuck in this pattern.

This succession of reactions is the reason why we might wonder why we don't have a clear direction. When we only deal with *Urgent*, we don't build. We just manage interruptions. Sometimes these interruptions are very *Important*, and sometimes not. When we spend our time on what matters to us, we are able to achieve our goals.

I created a simple exercise that will give you an instant picture of where you are going. You will need a pen and three different colors of post-its. For the purpose of this example, let's pretend my post-its are purple, blue, and yellow.

On the purple post-it pad, write your five most important values, what matters to you, and what you strongly believe in—one value per post-it. It can be "helping others," "staying healthy," "being a person of integrity," "making money," "succeeding at school," "spending time with friends," "spending time with family,"…

On the blue post-it pad, write your five most important goals, what you want to achieve and reach—one value per post-it. It can be "getting promoted," "opening my own business," "starting a family," "learning a new language," "developing new friendships," "creating a balance between work and life," "owning my home,"…

On the third post-it pad, write where you spend most of your time, look at your daily routine and write down five items—one value per post-it. It can be "working," "exercising," "hanging out with friends," "practicing an instrument," "watching TV," "reading the news," "posting on a particular social media," "studying,"…

Put all the post-its on your table. Then try to match a goal with a value and a time spent.

Example:

Goal: being fit

Value: staying healthy

Time: exercising

Every match is a direction. If you cannot match a particular goal with a value and time spent, this goal won't happen in your reality. Either you don't really believe in it, or you are not investing your time in this goal.

Sometime we are just spending our time.

 "It's not that we have a short time to live, but that we waste a lot of it." —Rebbe

Take the time to write down what you just learned about yourself before going to the next page.

_____

_____

_____

_____

_____

_____

_____

_____

_____

_____

_____

_____

_____

_____

_____

_____

# Do not confuse *Investing* time with *Spending* time

**W**hen it comes to time, aim to think about *Investing* it, not *Spending* it.

When you invest your time in your relationship with your spouse, you have a good marriage. When you invest your time studying, you enhance your brain. When you invest your time with your child, you develop the parent in you.

Where you spend and invest your time will determine your future. Your future is the result of organizing your time in the present.

We all have 24 hours in a day. The secret is how you orient this time.

"What you invest your time in defines who you are." —Todd Duncan

# Do not confuse
# *Essential* with *Optional*

**W**hat do I need in my life to be happy? Order.

It is interesting how often the word order can have a negative connotation and be associated with rigidity.

Order actually creates the opposite of rigidity. With order you don't go with the flow. You organize a structure to manage the flow and direct your energy towards essentiality - not superficiality.

Think about the house of your dreams for example.

When you think about it, you picture yourself happy in it. You can see clearly the colors of the wall, the kitchen countertop, the chandelier in the bedroom, the garden, the fireplace… Unless you are the architect, you don't picture the time to build strong foundations under the ground, the insulation system…

Now let's rewind.

You picture yourself happy. You are happy because what you are seeing is your home, not just a house. A home is a structure, and the house is what is built around it. Spending time on the structure is spending time on what is essential.

You picture yourself happily cooking with your loved ones in a beautiful kitchen. Focus on building kindness, patience, perseverance, compassion, humility, rigor, and harmony. Don't start with the color of the countertop, it won't get you where you want to go.

"Photography does deal with "truth" or a kind of superficial reality better than any of the other arts, but it never questions the nature of reality – it simply reproduces reality. And what good is that when the things of real value in life are invisible?" —Duane Michaels

# Do not confuse
# *Control* with *Respect*

Take the time to think about what *Respect* means to you. If someone does not obey you, does this mean this person is being disrespectful to you? If someone doesn't give you what you asked for, does this mean they are being disrespectful to you?

When we operate in crisis mode, our only goal is to control the situation. We only care about the urgency of the problem. Our focus is not on the people involved in it. Nor the discussions. We don't even seek clarification.

On the other hand, we have to treat others the way we want to be treated in life.

Now let's take the time to think about how we want to be treated. Do we want to be rushed? Do we want to be yelled at? Do we want to be understood? Do we want the people around us to show us more possibilities?

Every time we start a new relationship, we have the opportunity to discover more and more about how we want to be treated. And in this process of discovery, we adjust our boundaries while understanding those of others.

 "If your goal is to try to control people, they will eventually try to control you." —Me

# Do not confuse
# *Boundaries* with *Limitations*

Sometimes, you need to say "no". And it is perfectly fine. It actually is very healthy. "No, I cannot do it now, I will do it later," or "no, I cannot do it." It takes practice, but it is essential to your well-being. Saying no helps you articulate the difference between my needs and your needs. Between my space and your space. Between my time and your time.

Saying no builds the respect and self-esteem that everyone needs. The way the person receives your "no" is not your problem. They will figure it out. You cannot please everyone. That should not be your goal. Your goal is to build healthy *Boundaries*.

*Limitations*, on the other hand, are internal. They regulate our relationship with ourselves. What you think you can do, cannot do, deserve, don't deserve… It can be a long list.

Limitations love to hide behind our self-talk. It feels great to get them out of our system once we are done playing hide and seek with them.

Then the sky is the limit.

Destroy your own *Limitations*, not your *Boundaries*.

Build *Boundaries* and respect the *Boundaries* that others build. This way, you will learn how to receive and not just take from people.

"You can do anything as long as it is moral. The only limitations that you should keep are in your moral compass." —Me

# Do not confuse
# *Taking* with *Receiving*

**M**ost relationships are about giving and taking. Now that we spoke about *Boundaries*, you might understand why *Giving* and *Receiving* is actually a healthier way to look at a relationship.

*Receiving* is accepting.

*Receiving* builds trust in the relationship. *Receiving* happens when two people are approaching a relationship at the same level. No one is trying to control the other one. No one is trying to take advantage of anyone. No one wins, and no one loses. The relationship is developing in a way that allows the participants to respect one another. They are both engaged in the relationship.

*Receiving* acknowledges that there is a relationship.

It can take time to learn to receive and not to take. But it builds strong and healthy relationships. I accept what is there, including my frustration. When we receive, we build gratitude.

When we take, we create endless needs for ourselves and are seldom satisfied.

Gratitude is a feeling that brings Joy.

"Go where you are celebrated, and not tolerated, this is the art of becoming your greatest version." —Ralph Smart

# Do not confuse
## *Joy* with *Pleasure*

*P*leasure is a movement towards me. It varies according to outside stimuli that are things. It can be sugar, alcohol, adrenaline. You name it. *Pleasure* concerns the body and its limitations. That's why *Pleasure* is limited.

No matter how many pleasures you add, that will never result in *Joy*.

The pursuit of *Pleasure* reinforces hedonism. Not happiness. Choosing to invest your energy to seek out one pleasure after another might take you down a road that puts you in danger. And the insatiability that arises with *Pleasure* can lead us to seek out many parallel lives.

On the contrary *Joy* is not something we seek out, rather it is an emotion that arises within us. A movement from me to the world. I feel connected. This connection creates *Joy* - inside and outside. It does not feed our hunger for *Pleasure*; it fulfills us. As such, we form a rock-solid foundation for our life.

With true internal *Joy* we feel like building this one life where we can have everything.

"What can I get" no longer drives our behaviors and makes the decisions for us. Instead, we focus on "what contribution can I make."

In the early seventies, an experiment was conducted by Walter Mischel on children 5 to 6 years old called "the marshmallow test". They were given one marshmallow and two options: either they could eat the marshmallow now, or, if they waited 10 minutes before eating it, the researcher would come back with a second marshmallow for them. They were left alone in a room with the marshmallow for 10 minutes while the researchers observed their behaviors.

The idea behind this experiment was to see how children could delay gratification.

In this equation, one marshmallow = *Pleasure*, two marshmallows = *Happiness*. One marshmallow = impulse, two marshmallows = decision. If we jump at the chance to enjoy just the one marshmallow *Pleasure* is finite, and we are likely left wanting more. Suppose we are, however, able to wait for a second one. In that case, we are freed from impulse through our decision which is actually liberating. Now we are talking about *Joy*.

The easiest way to know if we are talking about *Pleasure* or *Joy* is to check in with our intention.

"The Joy that arises from being able
to overcome this obstacle surpasses
the Pleasure that we receive by eating
the marshmallow itself." —Me

# Do not confuse
# *I want* to with *I*
# *would love* to

*I* *want to* comes directly from the soul, at full power.

This energy allows you to overcome any obstacle along the way. It works with any project that you will consider, and any relationships. Some people call it commitment, others call it dedication. Whichever way you call it, you are engaging your full self.

*I want to* is actually an invitation to grow. You are bringing into your reality what is important to you. The strength that you develop through this process is endless.

*I would love to,* however implies curiosity but no real intention.

Chances are, you might give up at the first obstacle that will come along the way. You are curious to satisfy a *Pleasure*. To take. But not necessary to give or to invest. *I would love to* refers to what I can possibly gain from a particular situation.

I don't put my heart into it. Usually the next question is: is it worth all these efforts?

A project that starts with *I would like to* usually finishes with "I didn't ask for this" or "that's not what I was hoping for". *I would love to* and *Hope* go hand in hand.

 "Don't judge yourself by immediate results, there are no shortcuts to any place worth going." —Mendel Kalmenson

# Do not confuse
# *Trust* with *Hope*

Sometimes we start to be curious about a project, start working on it, and *Hope* it will work out. We hope that it will bring the result that we need. And if it doesn't, we start experiencing all kinds of emotions: frustration, surprise...

Our focus is only on the result. And the way to get there is built with *Hope*.

Sometimes we think about a project and put all our effort into it. And we accept that no matter the outcome, we will feel ok because we know that our intention is at its best. Our focus is on our efforts and how we are thinking about approaching this project. Our focus is on what we have control over. We learn to stay present and trust the process. We understand that we are developing capabilities and traits that we would not have developed otherwise.

As a result, we are able to bring our best selves into reality, and we are investing a part of ourselves in this experience - A seed. This seed will become Strength.

 "The day you plant the seed is not the day you eat the fruit." —Matt Hogan

# Do not confuse
# *Tough* with *Strong*

*T*ough does not need to care. *Tough* is tactical, and it needs to win. There is no flexibility in *Tough*. It is a way to respond to what is happening.

*Strength* comes from inside of us, and it is something that we build. We build it when nothing goes as expected when we go through difficult times. We build it when everything around us gets uncertain. But we keep going because we know there is something better on the other side of this uncertainty.

Strength is infinite and powerful. It radiates.

When we build *Strength*, we are in the position to influence others.

We don't need to force anything.

"When nothing goes right... go left!" — Martha Cecilia

Spend as much time as possible on finding what you want to achieve. Know that there will be moments of discouragement along the way. But once your vision is clear, if you start doubting yourself, revisit the steps, not the direction.

Truly believe you have the *Strength*; you just need to rethink the approach without letting your ego get in the way.

Our ego loves to be upset about the immediate results.

That's why we need to keep it busy when things don't go as expected. Then we can stay focused on a new approach. It brings stability and helps create certainty for us and our loved ones.

This is what *Strength* looks like. *Strength* moves you forward.

 "When it is obvious that the goals cannot be reached, don't adjust the goals, adjust the action steps." —Confucius

# Do not confuse
# *Change* with *Transformation*

*C*hange is tactical. *Change* is in the moment. And, like any reaction, it is oriented towards a situation.

I decide to Change my schedule to exercise every morning because I feel tired and want to do something about it. I start, and after a week, I go back to my old habits.

What happened? I was reacting to a frustration. When the feeling went away, there was no motivation behind it.

Our emotions are volatile. That's why we should think twice before making decisions with them.

When we take the time to observe, receive and identify them, we can then make a decision with our minds.

*Transformation* is a more robust power because it has deeper, long-lasting roots. I want to exercise because it is good for me. Now I am ready to take baby steps to achieve this goal. *Transformation* is about a belief.

Every situation around us creates an opportunity for us to refine ourselves. It's our duty. If we focus on the idea that we cannot change a situation, but we can transform our approach, we can fully develop who we are and unlock our potential.

We are no longer trying to refrain from feeling a particular emotion. We are welcoming this emotion and then checking in with our core values.

What is important to me?

When my neighbor is bothering me with the noise that he sometimes makes, he is actually allowing me to practice controlling my reaction. When I have to wait in line, I practice patience. When the train is late, I practice anticipation. I have to be in constant awareness that I can develop a trait and grow with any given situation.

"The one that I am
interacting with is my test."
—Rav Yehia Benchetrit

Set out life.

Stand at highest point.
What is your purpose
What gives your life meaning

What if I looked out
beyond this life?

Heading toward death
what .. brings life meaning.

*love this*

# Do not confuse
# *Existing* with *Living*

*Living Bigger*
*wild me*
*I would to loud –*

**E**xisting is fulfilling basic needs. I need to eat, I need to drink, I need to sleep... Focusing on my needs is actually not fun at all. Where will I find the energy to do all of this?

*Existing* can be oppressive. The focus is on me, and it is very limiting. It weakens my system.

*Living* is about purpose and meaning. It connects us to a bigger project than taking care of daily necessities. *Living* elevates us because our focus is on what is happening outside of us and the impact we can have.

*Existing* is learning to drive a car. Everyone is looking at me: the instructor, myself... Even the pedestrians seem to be looking at me.

*Living* is going on the road. My eyes, focus, and intentions are outside of my system. I have already internalized that I need to put my seat belt, check the mirrors, to turn the key… I can now focus on the road.

I am using the car for what it is. A way of traveling. Not my destination. But I needed the car to become a driver. And I needed to become a driver to go on the road.

Now I cannot wait to create the itinerary for my journey!

Once you have experienced *Living*, you cannot simply go back to *Existing* - precisely because you understand the extraordinary impact you can have on others.

 "Invest yourself in a bigger purpose and you will never feel empty." —Me

# Do not confuse
# *Window Shop* with *Bait*

**H**ave you ever looked at something in a *Window Shop* attracting you? Then what happens next? You enter the shop excited about the idea that you will find more of what you liked in the window.

Sometimes you find even more interesting things than in the Window Shop.

And it is a wonderful surprise. And sometimes you realize that the only thing you like, now that you are in the shop, is actually what was in the Window Shop. The rest is totally different. It can be unpleasant.

It is like the *Window* was a *Bait*, and you fell for it.

The concept is the same apropos of us human beings. Our private and public persona can sometimes be complete opposites without us realizing it. Being aware of this possible gap is very important for the quality of our relationships.

We live better when our *Shop* and our *Window Shop* represent the same reality. Trying to mask our true selves to fit in will eventually prevent us from feeling connected. To us. To others. No one needs this stress.

"Focus on understanding who you really are. Appreciate it. It will radiate all the way through the Window Shop." —Me

- CHARGING STATION 4 -

# Clarity in actions brings movement in life

Freedom is back, it's time to see what it looks like!

According to the Oxford Languages Dictionary, "freedom is the power or right to act, to speak, or think as one wants without hindrance or restraint."

How, if I can do whatever I want, do I create certainty? And how can I prevent myself from falling into a reckless behavior?

To be at peace with freedom - funny to think about it this way - we need to consider two things: the way we manage ourselves and the goal towards which we are moving.

As we saw earlier, managing ourselves is synchronizing in our system our thoughts, our words and our actions. It is a daily practice. And our results will be proportionate to the compassion that we show towards ourselves. No one woke up and decided to run a marathon, read about it, understood everything that it takes and just did it. No matter how much time we spend learning and understanding a concept, it is when we start practicing it that it becomes a reality.

Compassion is the key to perseverance. And perseverance is the key to becoming what we learned.

The next question is: where do I want to put all my energy?

This question is meant to determine our goal by checking with our true intention. What is the impact that I want to have? On which cause?

Freedom is actually not "I do what I want whenever I want wherever I want with whomever I want".

Freedom is creating my own path without feeling limited by others or by myself. Freedom is expanding my mind while respecting the boundaries of others. So that, they too can experience freedom.

Freedom is not me alone. Freedom is me with others. That's why now, we need to look at relationships.

## What makes a relationship?

According to the Oxford Languages Dictionary, "a relationship is the way in which two or more concepts, objects, or people are connected, or the state of being connected."

In crisis mode, we mostly work on the relationship at a transactional level. The interaction starts with a need and ends with a consequence." If I do that, I will get that", "if I don't do that, I will be able to avoid this"… There is always an agenda behind every interaction. We need to manage the risk. It's like participating in a giant dodgeball game. The focus is on where the ball is and is not supposed to be. There is a beginning and an end to the game and we keep the score. And the score determines how good we are. Not the way we treat people. There is only the ball.

And this ball is often a personal or professional project with deadlines involving a lot of different people.

In living mode though, what I think of me and what others think of me will influence my behavior and ultimately my performance. And that's only on my end. Everyone is also evolving at their own pace because everyone is trying to develop their unique character.

There are lots of moving parts.

I can find myself dealing with someone who says he will do something, but does not. I can find myself interacting with someone who is forgetting important details about a project and does not see that it creates confusion. Not to mention that sometimes this person can be me.

## What is my goal?

My goal is to finish this project in time with the best possible interactions.

If I focus on proving to people around me that they are wrong, chances are, next project, when I am wrong, they will surely let me know. And we are going to spend a lot of time talking about it.

The result will occur in the space where I designate my focus.

If I let the relationship improvise itself and react, I will lose sight of my initial goal. If I put my focus on moving forward with our agenda, it will happen.

If I have too much work, I can delegate. If I am confused I can ask for clarifications. Asking for clarifications does not mean I am stupid; it means that I want to move forward. And it might be because my colleague is not clear or I missed some part of what a colleague said.

Nevertheless, right now, I am stuck, and my goal is not to blame anyone; my goal is to move forward.

Clarifying is very often part of the solution.

Confusion creates misunderstandings, and misunderstandings creates conflicts. And with conflicts, we feel discouraged, which then creates inertia.

Clarifications hold a very important part in working and living together. They get us closer to our goal. When I clarify my expectations with someone, it helps me clarify my own thinking. It creates a good channel for healthy communication. It creates a natural drive. Everyone is energized and contributing.

The goal is now to remain engaged despite the obstacles along the way. Shall we have a look at endurance?

# What place does endurance have in our lives?

According to the Oxford Languages Dictionary, "endurance is the fact or power of enduring an unpleasant or difficult process or situation without giving way".
Endurance is "staying with the problem" and accepting that we will feel uncomfortable until we can think of an acceptable solution.

In crisis mode we practice endurance without realizing it. We don't have a choice with the reality in front of us.

Our goal is to push our limits.

"Never enough" is our way of living. It is never enough, and we are never enough. We are constantly practicing giving everything that we have. We are continually pushing something outside of our system. And it serves us very well.

When we are ready to *build* our lives, we use the same determination that we have inside of us but we orient it differently.

We are not working "against" but rather "with" our surroundings. It is not everything or nothing. Our capacity to manage our stress is a key component of our success. As well as to accept that not everyone thinks like us. That's why we put our focus on the relationship. And we try to focus less on our ego.

Our focus is on how our behavior will affect positively or negatively our interactions. Can I see beyond this particular project? Why do people enjoy working with me beyond the fact that I get the work done? Do I allow them to grow and develop new skills? Do they feel comfortable sharing their ideas with me?

We can't stay only in our minds. We need to get out of ourselves and be more aware of what is happening around us.

## What is it about awareness?

According to the Oxford Languages Dictionary, "awareness is the knowledge or the perception of a situation or fact".

There is a *To-do list* in every situation that we face, and there is a *To-be list*.

The idea is that as soon as we realize that we cannot do anything about the events, we switch into the *To-be list* mode.

Let's imagine I am in my car, on my way home. Something unexpected happens, and I am stuck in traffic. It doesn't look good.

Even if I am very skilled at improvising, my skills won't do much right now. I cannot change this situation, and I cannot ask my car to become a plane. Once I have accepted that, no matter what I do, I cannot change the fact that I cannot move my car, I can start thinking of how I can, in fact, *be* about this situation.

I need to switch to my *To-be list*.

On my *To-do list*, I was supposed to arrive home at a particular time. That was the task that I was ready to check off.

On my *To-be list* now, I see that I have to avoid creating an argument with people around me because of the stress of not being able to do what was expected of me.

And the good news is that I have total control over that.

Map of relationships
+ phone
+ worth.

# Relationships

Picture yourself traveling to the destination of your dream. Your luggage is packed; you are ready and excited, and your sunglasses are already on your nose. The taxi comes to pick you up. Today is your lucky day; you were able to get this new generation of taxis that has the ultimate self-driving system. You feel so safe. Not to mention the fact that you don't like to talk before your third coffee, so, with no driver in sight, it is really looking good. The car starts moving; there is no traffic, and the road is clear and open. It is what perfection looks like.

At the first intersection, the taxi stops at a 7-Eleven. The voice in the taxi asks you if you would like to check what is available there, to make sure you won't be missing anything for your trip. You didn't ask for it but thinking about it; you might need some gum and coffee. You finish paying and get back into the car. You are now on the road again. Ready.

You arrive at a second intersection, and the taxi stops again in front of another 7-Eleven. The voice asks if you would like to check what is available there if you need something for the trip. You feel that you have everything, including a great mood, and don't really need anything. But, whatever, you get out of the car, buy water, and get back in the car. The vehicle is moving again. You are now picturing yourself happy in this beautiful destination, while at the same time starting to feel a little anxious, realizing that you might arrive late at the airport.

That's when the taxi stops for the third time, at the third intersection and the third 7-Eleven. The voice is asking if you would like to check what they have in case you might need something for the trip. At that point, you are starting to be a little upset. You start talking to "the" voice: "Listen, I am sorry, but I don't think I need anything right now. Thank you so very much. When I need something, I am sure we will find a 7-Eleven. The 7-Eleven will always be open; that's why we call them 7-Eleven. They are everywhere. Now please, I don't want to stop again. I have somewhere to be."

That's when the voice actually answers: "I totally get it. Maybe you don't need anything, but how about a little distraction? They have magazines and games and other great stuff too". Before I can think of anything, the voice finishes by saying: "It's fine, really, I will wait for you."

Now, I am stressed. I realize that this voice will not listen to anything that I have to say. After all, this voice does not have ears and has all the time in the world, but I don't. I think I am better off getting into another taxi. Maybe this time, I will start by telling the taxi driver that I don't want to stop anywhere between here and the airport. Once this is established, I will be more relaxed.

As you understood, in this story, the voice in the taxi is playing the role of your notifications. The taxi represents your phone, the 7-Eleven stops are all the apps, the airport is your potential, and your flight is what you are supposed to do with this potential. Your take-off.

The primary relationship that we have in life is the one with our phones. And the funny thing is that even though our phones are very talkative, we actually don't have real conversations with them. And they love to take us to places that are open 24/7.

But these phones have a lot to offer. This relationship can be different when we take the time to think about it. Maybe we can ask them for what we need - only when we need something. We can organize a time that works for us like we do when grocery shopping.

We're not open 24/7. That's what makes us human.

The relationship with our phones is actually significant. It directly impacts our ability to bring what we have to offer to the world. If there is one person we should bring to couple's therapy, it is our phone.

When we establish priorities ahead of time, we can build a life filled with everything we want to achieve.

Our life is made of many relationships. A relationship with ourselves, a relationship with a partner, a relationship with work, a relationship with our family, a relationship with our friends, a relationship with an organization we are invested in.

Interactions are part of these relationships, but they are not the relationship itself. The relationship is a project. The interactions help us achieve this project. We cannot interact with everyone around us thinking that we are building relationships when, in fact, we are playing ping pong with everyone.

Let's have a look at my interactions in a particular relationship.

Let's decide that the vision that I have of my relationship with work includes a goal for a balanced life. Am I working towards this goal if I find myself answering or sending professional emails at 10:00 PM? The project is a balanced life, and now I need to create the interactions that will help me bring this project into my reality. I start with one interaction and see how I can change it. I can decide that after X:00 PM, I am not sending or responding to any professional emails. And I practice it until it becomes a routine. If there is a situation at work, I will receive a phone call. I can now be fully present for myself, my friends, my hobby, and my family.

When we manage our interactions, we can avoid having everyone in our taxi simultaneously. Having everyone in our taxi at the same time creates noise and confusion. And we want quality time in each relationship.

Now that I have set out to manage interruptions and interactions, I can look at my relationship with my reality.

In this relationship, what is needed of me is to be constantly compatible with my reality. I need to invest time in preparing myself on the outside and the inside. So that when a situation happens, I am ready to handle it. Without swinging into reaction mode.

Let's imagine that I want to have a more prominent family, and I know that my future reality will need me to show more patience. Can I start developing more tolerance now, in my current reality? Let's imagine that I want to make some progress and become a better person. Can I start developing now more compassion towards myself? This project is very dear to my heart that I want to finish. Can I start developing more perseverance now? I want to have a healthier life in the future. Can I start developing more courage to let go of a bad habit? I am constantly getting ready in my current reality for my future reality.

Everything is in me. I just need to water these seeds.

When I move forward to my reality to adjust my traits, I feel that I am where I am supposed to be. And it is a great feeling! I feel compatible, I feel whole, and I feel alive.

On the opposite side, when I detach myself from what is required of me in my reality, I create space for fear and doubt. And those two love to make bad decisions for me. They feed themselves on illusions and have this unique ability to open parallel worlds for me, creating parallel lives. And I end up spending my time between these different lives instead of being between my current reality and my future reality.

By adjusting my traits to reality, I become myself. And I can move freely.

"Ultimately what you do is secondary. But how you do it is primary." —Eckhart Tolle

The *To-be list* is endless but is energizing in opposition to the *To-do list*.

I am not depleting myself; I am completing myself.

The good news is that I will never be able to finish my *To-be list*, and I am at peace with it. The goal of a *To-do list* is just to check off each new item as soon as I put it on the list. I don't think I need that stress.

The goal of a *To-be list* is to think of more items that I can work on. You can do many things in life and become nothing. With a *To-be list* you are guaranteed to become yourself. And things will get done without you realizing it. The *To-be list* is about refining myself and constantly working on many different traits. Every situation gives me this opportunity.

It is about becoming better instead of achieving more or reaching perfection.

A *To-be list* is very personal and unique, just like each of us. You can personalize your *To-be list* at the end of this book. And practice it.

"The grass is greener where you water it." — Wolfgang Puck

Inside of us, we have everything. We just need to be curious about ourselves. When our goal is to become our best selves, we soon realize that we will never be afraid to lose anything. We cannot lose what we have become.

The future is the present organized. When we organize our present, we will be satisfied with our future.

"When you become comfortable with uncertainty, infinite possibilities open up in your life." —Eckhart Tolle

Enjoy your life!
Stéphanie

# - My personal notebook -

My Alignment Clock

My Relationship Builder

My *To-Be List*

My Decistion Roundabout

# - My Alignment Clock -

## One situation at a time

**M**y alignment clock is a tool to help me observe what is not in alignment in my system. When a I feel a tension in myself and I feel pulled in different directions, it is time to check in with myself to find what is not in alignment.

Before

FULLY CHARGED

After

## Situation 1:

I was thinking _____

_____

_____

I said _____

_____

_____

I did _____

_____

_____


## Situation 2:

I was thinking _____

_____

_____

I said _____

_____

_____

I did _____

_____

_____

## Situation 3:

I was thinking _____

_____

_____

I said _____

_____

_____

I did _____

_____

_____

## Situation 4:

I was thinking _____

_____

_____

I said _____

_____

_____

I did _____

_____

_____

## Situation 5:

I was thinking _____

_____

_____

I said _____

_____

_____

I did _____

_____

_____

# - My Relationship Builder -

## one relationship at a time

Me              Interactions           Relationship

Me                       Interactions                   Relationship

                FULLY CHARGED

My relationship with

_____

_____

_____

My vision of this relationship

_____

_____

_____

_____

_____

What is the first interaction to create this vision

_____

_____

_____

_____

_____

My relationship with

_____

_____

_____

My vision of this relationship

_____

_____

_____

_____

_____

What is the first interaction to create this vision

_____

_____

_____

_____

_____

My relationship with

_____

_____

_____

My vision of this relationship

_____

_____

_____

_____

_____

What is the first interaction to create this vision

_____

_____

_____

_____

_____

My relationship with

_____

_____

_____

My vision of this relationship

_____

_____

_____

_____

_____

What is the first interaction to create this vision

_____

_____

_____

_____

_____

My relationship with

_____

_____

_____

My vision of this relationship

_____

_____

_____

_____

_____

What is the first interaction to create this vision

_____

_____

_____

_____

_____

# - My *To-Be* List -

one interaction at a time

**H**ere is a list of traits to get you started. They are not in any particular order and you can add other traits at the end of this list to make it yours. Take the time to look at it before starting to fill out your journal.

| | |
|---|---|
| Committed | Trustworthy |
| Loyal | Humble |
| Opened | Hard worker Courageous |
| Optimist | Generous |
| Spiritual | Determined |
| Kind | Fair |
| Accepting | Patient |
| Focused | Confident |
| Responsible | Polite |
| Honest | Reliable |
| Able to show empathy | Compassionate |
| Respectful | Disciplined |
| Perseverant | Understanding |
| Grateful | Caring |
| Curious | Able to demonstrate integrity |
| Flexible | Conscientious |
| True | _____ |
| _____ | _____ |
| _____ | _____ |

For each interaction that you had/have, you have the possibility to identify the trait in progress.

Interaction opportunity with

_____

_____

_____

_____

Context

_____

_____

_____

Trait in progress

_____

_____

_____

_____

Interaction opportunity with

_____

_____

_____

_____

Context

_____

_____

_____

_____

Trait in progress

_____

_____

_____

_____

Interaction opportunity with

_____

_____

_____

_____

Context

_____

_____

_____

_____

Trait in progress

_____

_____

_____

_____

Interaction opportunity with

_____

_____

_____

_____

Context

_____

_____

_____

_____

Trait in progress

_____

_____

_____

_____

Interaction opportunity with

_____

_____

_____

_____

Context

_____

_____

_____

_____

Trait in progress

_____

_____

_____

_____

Interaction opportunity with

_____

_____

_____

_____

Context

_____

_____

_____

_____

Trait in progress

_____

_____

_____

_____

Interaction opportunity with

_____

_____

_____

_____

Context

_____

_____

_____

_____

Trait in progress

_____

_____

_____

_____

Interaction opportunity with

_____

_____

_____

_____

Context

_____

_____

_____

_____

Trait in progress

_____

_____

_____

_____

# - My Decision Roundabout -

## one decision at a time

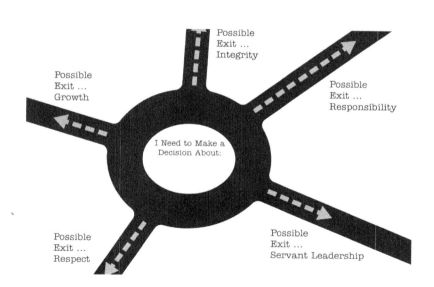

**O**ur values represent what's important for us. Each individual has their own set of values for life and for work.

We are building our decision roundabout every time we are consulting with our values before making any decision.

Look at the list of these five core values below.

Write your decision in the center of the circle and then ask yourself these five questions to make your decision. Each door can open with a simple yes. Each door will stay closed with a no.

Now try to find two doors from which your decision can exit and exist!

# Values for your Decision Roundabout

## INTEGRITY

Would I do the same if no one was looking at me right now?

## RESPECT

Will this decision demonstrate my ability to treat others the way I want to be treated?

## RESPONSIBILITY

Will I be able to accept the consequences without blaming anyone?

## GROWTH

Will this decision open possibilities for me or others to grow?

## SERVANT LEADERSHIP

Will this decision serve a bigger purpose than my own self?

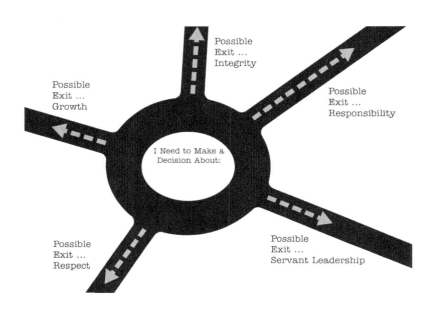

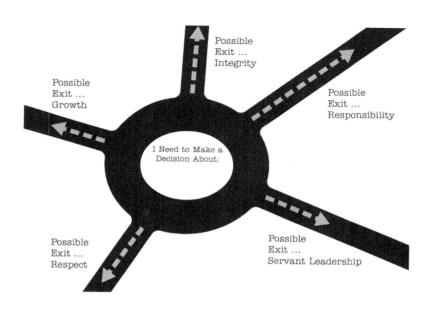

Possible Exit ... Integrity

Possible Exit ... Responsibility

Possible Exit ... Growth

I Need to Make a Decision About:

Possible Exit ... Respect

Possible Exit ... Servant Leadership

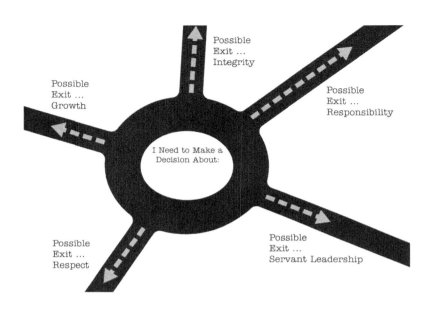

Possible
Exit ...
Integrity

Possible
Exit ...
Responsibility

Possible
Exit ...
Growth

I Need to Make a
Decision About:

Possible
Exit ...
Respect

Possible
Exit ...
Servant Leadership

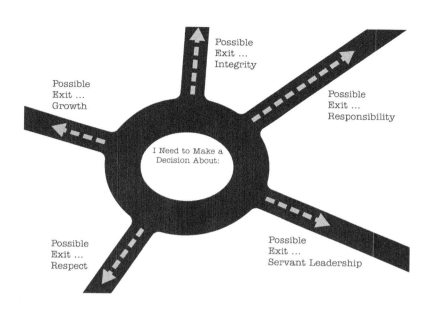

Possible
Exit ...
Integrity

Possible
Exit ...
Growth

Possible
Exit ...
Responsibility

I Need to Make a
Decision About:

Possible
Exit ...
Respect

Possible
Exit ...
Servant Leadership

# Acknowledgements

The first time I read a book from Dr Abraham Twerski was over 10 years ago. After that, I think that I read all his books again and again. He was a very special soul and he certainly contributed to inspire me in becoming a better person.

I would like to thank Rav Yehiah Benchetrit. I cannot count the number of classes that I attended but I can certainly count my blessings. I learned so much about life, relationships and values. Not to mention that he has a great sense of humor. He is the one who made me understand that I could learn a concept and had it very clear in my mind, but until I brought it to my heart, it was not in my system.

Finally, I would like to thank Rabbi Manis Friedman. His classes gave me a strong foundation for the third chapter of this book.

Through decades of coaching people, I heard one story after another. Each one more fascinating than the other one. Each story was unique just like each one of us. Even though all these people were very different, they were looking for the same thing: To feel alive, guilt-free and unstoppable.

Every time I am coaching someone, I am growing with this person. We are all connected, that's what makes us human.

This book is a thank you note for each person I had the honor to coach.

I want to thank Daniel for his edits.

I would like to thank Maya, Ileen, Amy, Cayle, Nicole, Stephy, Fatima, Elka for their comments, edits, suggestions and encouragement.

I thank my sister Nathalie for her support and unconditional love.

I want to thank my dear friends Ronn, Roey, Roy, Oded and Ariel.

I thank my three daughters for their love and patience when I was so busy editing this book for the 18th time. I love you.

Finally, I want to thank Meghan, Steve, Bob and the whole team at Best Seller Publishing.

Stéphanie

# Sources

**Yehia Benchetrit channel on Youtube**

- L'autre est mon épreuve
- Hasard et providence
- Avoir une feuille de route et s'y tenir
- Entier ou réfléchi,
- La parole et l'acte
- Le mensonge en vérité
- Le coeur centre de l'homme
- Temps relatif et temps absolu
- Sagesse de cœur
- Le couple qui et quoi
- La jalousie destructrice
- La capacité d'adaptation
- Peut-on changer

**Abraham Twerski channel on Youtube**

- Decision making
- Self-esteem
- How do lobsters grow
- Why the feeling of discomfort is so important
- Love

- Jealousy
- The purpose of life
- Attaining happiness
- How to never be angry again
- Depression
- Purpose
- How to never be stressed again
- How to improve your self-awareness and self-esteem

**Rabbi Manis Friedman channel on Youtube**

- Existing
- Happiness
- The comedy of marriage
- Stop trying so hard

**Links on the internet**

www.naia.org/champions-of-character/five-core-values

https://bettermarketing.pub/for-a-meaningful-life-choose-fulfillment-over-achievement-ca982c778a45

https://kidsnclicks.com/list-of-values

https://quotepark.com/quotes/1982111-ralph-smart-go-where-you-are-celebrated-not-tolerated-if-th

www.forbes.com/sites/amyblaschka/2018/09/04/every-thing-youve-ever-wanted-is-sitting-on-the-other-side-of-fear/?sh=e11a0d93979a

www.brainyquote.com/topics/superficial-quotes

www.google.com/search?q=spending+investing+-
time+quotes&sa=X&biw=893&bih=676&sxsrf=APq-WBs0x6N_
Z8ux4QdNWsnp8WbHrfHFZg:1646559997240&tbm=isch&-
source=iu&ictx=1&vet=1&fir=afL_NCrtA8q-4M%252C0som-
VX7tu-QwlM%252C_%253BwOHzZ1coyx2usM%252CVE1I_
GMXKBVWsM%252C_%253BEtfD2brLfQQXwM%252C0som-
VX7tu-QwlM%252C_%253BGQxOO_EUOpCdsM%252C-fi1G-
TOTbvsQiM%252C_%253BigvlYeC_WfDXJM%252C-alUT-
KLVt3u5SM%252C_%253BTQsYEiUEYU0QUM%252CVE1I_
GMXKBVWsM%252C_%253BxWie3VRaury0UM%-
252ClsQZYwJqSuByLM%252C_%253BiY5yN1XJYdfOp-
M%252C0somVX7tu-QwlM%252C_%253BhVHeOwd-
nUSkMJM%252C3u-dycQCzuFIxM%252C_%253B-rby-
i5cN-W5nXM%252C0somVX7tu-QwlM%252C_&us-
g=AI4_-kQ_oKKV-AB5Wat83pA4shsZgGgcpw&ved=2a-
hUKEwiAh_H9mbH2AhXYkIkEHX4nBioQ9QF6BAgTE-
AE#imgrc=GAi5BB24WBLlpM

www.quotemaster.org/passenger+seat

www.heartsandminds.org/inspire/decisions/?gclid=CjwK-
CAiA1JGRBhBSEiwAxXblwZdAPcMldEZjC6McwxRCH7em-
633hx_E2UF43EZLHZOCZXFzTrxkljBoCFSIQAvD_BwE

Printed in Great Britain
by Amazon